CHURCH SEARCH

How to Get Your Ministry to Show Up in Search Engines

KEVIN W. SHORTER

WestBow
PRESS

WestBow Press books may be ordered through booksellers or by contacting:

WestBow Press
A Division of Thomas Nelson
1663 Liberty Drive
Bloomington, IN 47403
www.westbowpress.com
1-(866) 928-1240

Because of the dynamic nature of the Internet, any Web addresses or links contained in this book may have changed since publication and may no longer be valid. The views expressed in this work are solely those of the author and do not necessarily reflect the views of the publisher, and the publisher hereby disclaims any responsibility for them.

ISBN: 978-1-4497-0107-9 (sc)
ISBN: 978-1-4497-0108-6 (e)

Library of Congress Control Number: 2010924407

Printed in the United States of America

WestBow Press rev. date: 04/02/10

Acknowledgements

My eternal gratitude to God who in His kind and unusual way encouraged me to write. May even a book about websites communicate your graciousness and love to your children.

To my wife, Allison, who believes in me and loves me even though she knows me so well. Thank you for your support throughout this process.

To Mir Haynes who proofread the early drafts for me. You are good partner to have. I would encourage anyone needing copywriting or copy proofing to check her out at AnaboStudios.com.

And finally to my daughters, Rachel and Elizabeth, who are perfect in every way.

Contents

Chapter 1

Why You Need to be Online and How

Two co-workers are talking at work. "My anniversary is coming up and I need to find a place to take my wife for dinner."

"A couple of years ago I went to this place with my wife. They had great food and atmosphere. My wife still talks about the piano playing while we ate."

"What was it called?"

"I don't remember. It was up in Huntersville."

"Here, let me Google it. Let's search for 'restaurant' and 'Huntersville' and 'piano.'"[1]

"Did you find it?"

"Was it called Mickey and Mooch?"

"That's it. You were able to find it?"

---

1   This search was performed on Google on 12/29/2007. Results may vary on a
    current search.

1

"I guess so. There's a write up on it on Citysearch. I guess it's still around. It's on Sam Furr Road. I know where that is. Let me write down that phone number in case that is where we go."

"Is there a link to their website?"

"Not on this page. Let me get back to Google. Hmm, there's no link on Google. Let me look at this review on AOL. There is a Mickey and Mooch page. And, okay, *there's* their website."

This conversation could have happened anywhere. Sure the business would be different and the search would have been for something else, but people everywhere are investigating new places online. Churches are no different.

Richard Reising, president of Artistry Marketing in Dallas, Texas, and author of the book Church Marketing 101, thinks "currently, 80 to 85 percent of people are finding their church based on websites… Websites are replacing the yellow pages as a key mode of church advertising."[2] This is exactly the point of this book. If the majority of church visitors determine which church to visit based on websites, you need to have your church's website findable online—or determine that visitors are not part of your outreach.

When most churches come across the stats from Mr. Reising or others stating the importance of an online presence, their response is to create an attractive website. Although web designers are great at their craft and can make nice websites, they generally do not consider whether people can find their works of art. Most web designers use Flash to create church websites—probably because they have been asked to do so—but search engines cannot read Flash so that content is now hidden from the rankings.

Calvary Baptist Church is arguably the largest church in Winston-Salem, NC. They have put time and money into creating a nice looking website, but if you search for "Church Winston Salem",

2   Dolan, Thomas G. "E-Curb Appeal" Your Church Magazine. November / December 2007. http://www.christianitytoday.com/yc/2007/006/4.30.html accessed 12/26/2007.

Calvary's website is ranked 34. Only a motivated seeker would look through that many pages to find you. Even a more refined church search "Baptist Church Winston Salem" ranks them at 10.[3] For Calvary, having a Flash-based site has hurt their website's walk-in traffic. The top three returns for this last search are not particularly beautiful sites, but search engines know what they are about.

Calvary is a wonderful church and was a church home to me for my first couple of years in Winston Salem. They have great people on staff and usually keep an eye on details. My guess is that they have someone watching the traffic to the site, which I also assume to be high. With 5,000 plus families as members and with many other regular attenders, they are bound to have large amounts of traffic. But, are they missing out on the traffic from people searching the internet for a church in Winston Salem? Are they missing out on the opportunity to speak to these searchers at a point when they are in touch with their felt need?

The goal of this book is to educate you on the importance of having a presence online for your church, how to leverage the power of search engines to help people find your online presence, and how to determine if people are viewing the pages you want them to view once they find your website. This book is not intending to take the place of the work of the Holy Spirit in drawing people to Jesus, and it is not intending to steal from the work of other ministries that your church is engaged in for the benefit of the body of Christ. Rather I desire that the tools you receive from this book would enable non-believers to stumble upon your church's website—to discover the work Christ is doing through your church and to be drawn to investigate further at your place of worship. Similarly, I hope this book will help Christians who have just moved to your area to more quickly find a church home by selecting some potentials through a few minutes online.

---

3 This search was performed on Google on 12/26/2007. Results may vary on a current search.

Remember, you never get a second chance to make a first impression. If you are not thinking with regards to search engine traffic, you might be leaving it up to other people to tell your story. Notice in the Mickey and Mooch example that the search performed led to reviews about the restaurant. Your church might have a great reputation, but are you going to rely solely on someone else to speak for you?

A BRIEF History of the Internet

The Internet began as a collection of social networks. Before there were web browsers, the Internet consisted of people making files available for storage and retrieval through the File Transfer Protocol (FTP). People and companies still use this process for files too large or too confidential for email.

The first search engine was created in 1990 by Alan Emtage, which he named Archie. Archie used a process that identified all anonymous FTP sites and then indexed all the files it found.

Around the same time, Tim Berners-Lee created the World Wide Web, the Internet's first web browser. In 1991 CERN, the European Organization for Nuclear Research, released the World Wide Web to the public and in 1993 it agreed to allow anyone to use web protocol and code royalty-free. In 1994 CompuServe, AOL, and Prodigy all began to provide Internet access, which is around the time most people started to hear about the Internet.

As web access became more available, more web pages were created.

Matthew Gray of MIT created the first acclaimed web robot. Robots have currently become the backbone of all search engines as they roam the Web visiting websites and collecting information about them. The misuse of some robots can actually slow your site down, if they access your site multiple times a day. Most search engines control their robots and allow for you to instruct them about what is important on your site.

Yahoo! came around in April 1994 and began cataloging websites into directories. The search feature on the site was initially the ability to search the Yahoo! directories. At that time, other search engines were just searching URLs, and if you browsed the web at that time, most URLs had nothing to do with a site's content. In fact, many URLs were just a collection of numbers strung together. Yahoo's directory had descriptive information about each website, allowing for better search.

In September 1998, Stanford students Larry Page and Sergey Brin became late entries to the search engine world with the creation of Google. These men had created the ability to quickly filter through thousands of databases worth of information to generate the desired response. The speed and search result relevance of Google quickly began to win over web users. As of May 2009, 73% of all Internet searching is done on Google. Yahoo! gains 16% of all searching, and Bing gets 6%. The increasing collection of other search engines fills in the rest.[4]

Google, and now most other search engines, have created tools known as "crawlers" or "spiders" that roam the web. Their job is to visit billions of websites, collect data and catalog source code. The more a site changes, the more often these spiders return to that site. Search engines take the information collected from the spiders to determine what you see in search rankings.

---

4   Data from Hitwise.com looking at four-week rolling periods. Compiled Sullivan, Danny "Hitwise: Bing Both Grows & Drops In June; Google Still Tops" search engine land. July 2009. http://searchengineland.com/hitwise-bing-both-grows-google-still-tops-22202 accessed 07/14/2009.

What Determines Search Ranking?

SEARCH ENGINE RANKING = Content + Links + Traffic + Unknown

How do search engines use the information that spiders collect? For the most part, this is the competitive advantage that search engine companies hold very tightly. In general, though, Search Engine Ranking = Content + Links + Traffic + Unknown. Search Engine Optimization (SEO) is the set of methods that are used to increase a website's ranking on web searches. There are three steps to effective SEO: keyword analysis, on-site integration and off-site optimization. Effective use of the latter two will increase your site's ranking for the keywords you have placed in your site.

Keyword Analysis: Every SEO company uses basically the same type of program to run the keyword analyses for the sites they are working on. The program will search the last three months of data from the top 10 search engines. The program allows the user to enter a set of keywords that describe the site. From those words, it generates a list of every possible combination of phrases that related to one of those keywords entered. Beside each phrase it would show how many searches per day are done. The program itself is a commodity; the value that an SEO firm offers (what the consultants get paid for) is in the interpretation of the data. If you hire an SEO firm to perform keyword research and they ever hand you a simple print-out from some program, that firm has not done their job properly.

On-Site Integration: On-site integration is generally where most people think SEO takes place. Once a keyword phrase is decided upon, it is integrated into the site in an effort to make the search engines think your site is relevant to that given keyword phrase. This integration is difficult because it requires the owners of the site to pick which keyword phrases they want to focus on. If you do not focus on just a few keywords, the search engines assume you do not know what your site is about and will therefore rank the site lower. The way to increase the number of keywords that relate to your site is to have additional content on other pages. Strategic use of additional pages is to focus on a separate keyword phrase per page. You can have one overreaching keyword for the entire site, but then expand the site's reach by integrating separate keywords on additional pages to the site.

Off-Site Optimization: Off-site optimization is commonly viewed as link love or link juice. The search engines see a link to your site as a vote for your site, and a site with more votes will help gain higher rank. Links from your site to other sites tell search engines that your site leads visitors to relevant information; that can also increase your site's ranking.

The "vote" gets weighted heavier if the linking site is deemed as trustworthy by the search engines. Directories are the cheapest and most efficient way for websites to increase this trust. Every site you want to optimize should be listed in DMOZ and Yahoo! DMOZ is free but takes time; ranking is also at the whim of the editors of the directory. Yahoo! has an annual fee, but paying the fee increases your likelihood of inclusion.

The best use of time for off-site optimization is article submissions to blogs. Blogs are viewed by search engines just as websites. An obvious approach is to have the pastors or ministry leaders start blogging, but this may not be practical if the time it takes for upkeep begins taking away from other strategic activities. Keep in mind, though, that posting to a blog does not need to take too long. View the pastor's blog as a church-family devotional—each post doesn't have to have "that awe factor." Ministry leaders should just be real, personal, and share what God is doing in their lives.

Use a free blog program like Blogger or WordPress as the platform for your blog and then fit the blog into your church's URL (your actual web address). No need to hire a professional for this; in a matter of hours, your blog can be up and running and you will have saved time and money. From your blog, try to link to your church's site and to things you talk about (books, organizations, conferences, etc.) as much as you can as this will keep the link juice flowing and help boost your ranking.

You can also look for opportunities to write posts for other websites. Submitting articles or guest posts helps your site's ranking by having another site give a quality link back to your site. Remember: Each article you submit should link back to your site, so make sure the author of the website you write for links back to you.

Content + Links + Traffic + Unknown

Let's look back at the equation for what goes into search engine ranking. What should you do to manage your site for these items? Content will be the on-site integration discussed above. Links will be the off-site integration. Traffic is the hardest to manage, but you could get people within your ministry to come to the site. Give them a reason to come regularly either through a blog or sermon downloads. Just as links are a vote for your site, visits are also considered as votes. If people frequently go to your site, the search engine would assume there must be something there worth sending people to see.

Where are We Going?

The goal of this book is to get your ministry or church's website visible on the search engines. This is not a sure-fire way to generate church growth. That is up the hand of God and your willingness and ability to follow His call for your ministry. There are many ministries that are truly being used by God and that are seeing lives changed for the better; unfortunately, unless you already attend that church, you have no way of knowing about all that God is doing there!

Think of your website as your opportunity to tell the world what God is doing through your church or ministry. This book gives plenty of ideas and approaches to grow your website's popularity. Do not feel you have to do each of the ideas presented. They are not for everyone. I encourage you to prayerfully consider what is discussed and seek what the Lord has for you.

With that said, there are many things that you can do one-time and just leave your site alone to work for you. My wife has a site like this. She is a mother of two young daughters and is very plugged into ministries in our church. She does want to put in the time and energy needed to upkeep her business website. Even so, the website continues to draw in qualified leads for her business because it was set up correctly in the beginning. A search on "Winston Salem Professional Organizer" or "Winston Salem Closet Designs" will bring up her ShorterDesigns.com website as number 1.[5]

There is no reason your church or ministry cannot get there as well without much effort. I pray this book will be a powerful and effective tool for all of the churches that God is already using.

---

5   This search was performed on Google on 8/1/2009. Results may vary on a current search.

Chapter 2

The Backbone of SEO

Internal Components:

KEYWORD ANALYSIS

Keyword analysis is the foundation of success in driving search engine (i.e. organic) traffic to your site. This is the step where you determine what terms people are searching for and what particular set of words could be relevant to people that are interested in you.

Wordtracker and Overture both have online resources to help determine popular search terms. I would suggest the first set of terms you search be your city and church. This will show you phrases you want to implement on your homepage so those directly looking for local churches can easily find you.

Once you've run a Wordtracker or Overture analysis, you'll be able to look through the resulting report.

What do the numbers tell me? When you look at a Wordtracker or Overture report, you'll see the number of times that a given search term was found in their respective databases. Wordtracker, for example, uses a database that contains searches for 60 days—more than 310 million of them. So the count is the number of times the term was used in the last two months in the search engines from which Wordtracker builds its database.

There are many other things you need to determine. For example, do people search your denomination by name or by acronym (e.g. Evangelical Free or EV Free)? If your church is in a city outside a larger one, how are people searching (e.g. for Smyrna, Nashville, or Davidson County)? Getting this right will help you get your ministry into the consideration set of someone's search.

Your site is another great resource for determining terms to go after. Looking through your web traffic will show you what phrases people used to find your site. Doing a search on those words will show you how you rank. Improving these rankings is usually an easy source of traffic.

For a more advanced use of keyword analysis, start thinking of other things people would be searching that can be comparable to your church. People searching for child care in your city are probably new to your area or could be new parents. These types of people are great candidates for trying a new church. Make sure your child care ministry ranks for this.

Do you have a crisis pregnancy ministry? Try to get ranked for terms that people might use to find the local Planned Parenthood and put relevant information on that webpage. Do you have a sports ministry? Figure out the terms people in your city search to find the league sports. This can really go on infinitely. The more terms you secure; the better able people are to find you.

> *Some words you want to make sure you go after*
> *are your church's name, your pastor's name,*
> *your top ministries, and local terms.*

One Word of Warning. This process does not take the place of the actual ministry. Word of mouth is still the best advertisement and this will grow with an effective ministry. The goal of search engine optimization is to be another source of free advertising.

Internal Components:

ON-SITE INTEGRATION

Once you have determined the keywords you want to target, the next step is to implement them on your site. Before we delve into the technical placement of keywords, the first thing to consider is content. The content on the site is what a visitor will see and if it does not match what they were searching they will not stay on your site. A positive user experience will lead to positive search results.

With that said here are the locations that most search engines look at to determine keyword relevance:

- URL — The actual web address
- Page Title — What appears in the browser bar
- Breadcrumbs — How to get back to the homepage
- Link Anchors — Text you click to go to another webpage
- Headings — Text in bold on the site
- Text — Actual content on the site
- Alt Tags — Text that appears when you hover over an image
- Metatags — Descriptive text within the code that robots read

URL: If at all possible, secure the name of your church or ministry as the URL. This is not only for search but also for branding. If your church name is University Presbyterian Church, then UniversityPres. org would be the best option for you. It is easy to remember and works well for print advertising. If this is your name however, then you are in the unfortunate position of fighting hundreds of other churches with the same name for a relevant URL. Adding your city to the end can be the best alternative URL. It is also easy to remember and can help you rank for search within your city.

Some people advocate the use of dashes within the URL, such as University-Pres-Orlando.org. There is no additional search benefit to this approach. For this example search engines can determine each of the three words whether or not you use the dashes. I tend to believe they are unnecessary unless it would be difficult to read the URL without it as in UPC-Orlando.org.

> *Why do I keep using .org instead of .com? The .org signifies you as a non-profit organization, but there is nothing set in stone that you have to use this ending. Since ministries seem to have adopted this as their own, my hunch is that you would be better off with a .org for your main ministry website, but if you do any outreach initiatives which you are using a separate microsite, then you might consider using a .com.*

Page Title: The page title is created within the webpage code under the <Title> tag. The main reason this is important is because it is what search engines use as the link text to your site in the rankings. If you search for "site:www.yoursite.org," you will see all the page titles to your site that are indexed by that search engine. A proper page title helps people know what that page is about.

I am a proponent of having every page start with your church name followed by what the specific page is about. For instance:

- Colonial Baptist Church: Cary, NC
- Colonial Baptist Church: Staff
- Colonial Baptist Church: Directions

- Colonial Baptist Church: Student Ministry
- Colonial Baptist Church: Sermons

Some people in the SEO industry advocate putting the keywords at the beginning of the title, and only if necessary add your site's name to the end. While this *may* give an additional boost in SEO, my marketing side still feels the presentation is better to list your name first. It looks cleaner, and you are up front about who you are. The other way seems, to me, as if you are trying to trick someone into visiting your site. But whatever you decide to do, the important thing is that each page has its own unique and descriptive page title.

Breadcrumbs: Breadcrumbs are an on-site map of how the page you are on links back to the homepage. This is a user-friendly technique that allows visitors to your site see how to navigate your site. The benefit for search is that the keywords in the breadcrumbs signal that your site is designated to these items. Each layer of the breadcrumb will lead you to that section, and the text for that layer is weighted heavily in the search algorithms.

Usually online shopping sites get this right—maybe because they live off of people finding what they are selling. Here are some examples of what some breadcrumbs look like:

- Target : Kids : Favorite Characters : Dora + Diego
- FamilyLife > Better Parenting > Why Everybody Loves Raymond
- MailChimp / Resources / Email Marketing Etiquette

Link Anchor Tags: A link anchor tag is the text used in the hyperlink to another page. This link will have relatively the same merit going either to another page on your site or to another site altogether. The greater benefit will go to the site to which the link is directed, but it does have added benefit to your page as well. Search engine writers believe that if you put a link on your site then your site must have some relevance to the text used in the link.

One way you can make this work for you is to keep an updated list of current events within your city, linking to the webpages for these events By this you can become the go-to source of activities in your area and rank your site for searches for "<<your city's>> activities." It would also give you a place to add your events while remaining relevant to people not going to your church. If you take this approach, please keep the events up-to-date. It negatively affects your site's credibility when you're promoting an up-coming event that happened months ago.

Headings: Headings are technically what you put in a <H1>, <H2>, or <H3> tag, but it works just about the same for anything in bold on your site. By making the text stand out, you are signaling that this word or phrase is important on this page. You must use this judiciously because an overuse of bold is not only distracting for a visitor to your site, but it is counted against you by search engines.

Text: Text is the copy on the website that visitors read. As a marketer by trade, I believe this part is too often ignored. The text gives your visitors a significant impression about who you are. What does your website say about your organization? Is your message easy to understand? Are there any errors on the page?

There are things that every ministry website should include: Your purpose, vision, core beliefs. Who is on staff? Where are you located? What services do you provide and when are they held? With this in mind, you should think through how you present and word this information. Reread what you write. Does it make sense? Have someone not related to your ministry read it. Do they understand what you mean? Pastors love to break the ice with reading mistakes in church bulletins (e.g. All women who are struggling trying to get pregnant see the pastor in his study after the service). Don't let your website be a joke in someone else's sermon!

With regards to SEO, text is very important. People use search engines to find the phrases they enter. If the phrase they enter is not somewhere in the text of the site, then your site must not really be about that phrase. This is where the early years of SEO failed. People used to think—and they used to be right—that all they needed to do was put key phrases in the code. Along the same lines, some people still try to hide text on the page by using a text color that is the same as the background. Both of these methods are strongly discouraged and, in some cases, will cause your site to be de-listed from search engines altogether.

The bottom line is: Make the content on the page relevant, informative and well-written. Sprinkle key phrases into the copy where they make sense so that people will be sure to find your webpages in their online searches.

Alt Tags: An alt tag is the text you can use to identify images. Search engines cannot read images so they use the alt tag to identify what the image is. Most people make the mistake of not using these markers and missing out on this benefit.

Some of the sites I manage get a large amount of traffic just from the image searches from search engines. This traffic might not translate to highly qualified leads to your site, but the more people that come to your site, the more opportunities you have to expose the vision and goals of your ministry.

While we are on the topic of images, churches and ministries should keep a photo record of events they hold. This is an easy way to add content that people want to see to your site. Stock photos are great for helping the site's main pages look professional, but someone investigating your church wants to see the types of people who are actually involved. Do the people at your church look like people they would be friends with? This is a huge hurdle for some people. And remember these images can create more incidental traffic to your site—just remember to use the alt tags.

Churches can also benefit from getting their members actively involved in providing pictures. You can create a section of your site for people to upload images and add their own descriptions. For your safety, you can create an approval process so that images are only pushed live after they have been approved by someone on staff.

Metatags: Metatags are snippets of code on your site that give search engines information about your site. This is the code I mentioned earlier—the stuff that people used to spend too much energy and time focusing on. Metatags *are* helpful to search engines because they provide details on what the page is about, but metatags are just one piece of the puzzle; they must be taken in context with everything else on the page.

You should put the metatags somewhere after the <head> tag and before the <body> tag. Here are some examples of metatags with descriptions.

<meta name="**description**" content="Meeting the spiritual needs of our city.">

Keep this to 150 characters telling what the site is about. Most of time the search engines will use this as the information in the link to your site, and they will cut it off at this limit. Make sure your city is in the description and that every webpage has a different description.

<meta name="**keywords**" content="keyword, another keyword, city, ministry, etc.">

Have no more than ten keywords separated by commas. Each page should be somewhat different, but your ministry name should be on every page.

<meta name="**URL**" content= "www.yourURL.org">

<meta name="**author**" content="Pastor">

The author tag is not really important, but it might help if you need help getting a name ranked.

<meta name="**copyright**" content="Copyright (c) 2009 Ministry Name">

<meta name="**googlebot**" content= "index,follow">

This tells Google to index your site and to follow its links. You will use noindex, nofollow if the page is anything you do not want people to find, like your stage site.

<meta name="**robots**" content= "index,follow">

Same as above but for other search engines.

<meta name="**revisit-after**" content="3 days">

This tells search engines how often you change the content on your page.

<meta name="**distribution**" content="global">

I am not sure the importance of this, but it is in use on some sites.

<meta name="**rating**" content="General">

This is used more for sites that have questionable content; by entering "General," you're stating that you do not have any adult content on your site.

EXTRA CREDIT

For the programmers in the bunch, you can make this process much easier by creating schemes that pull in the code to each page from databases. Databases can be updated easier with new page titles, headers, alt tags and metatags by updating a spreadsheet and allowing the database to update the webpages. It can save you a great deal of time if you can have someone set up your site with this functionality.

As we are discussing the coding, it is important to note that your site should be clearly coded. A clearly coded site allows the search engine robots to find what they need easily and, therefore, to more accurately index your site. W3C.org has links that can test your site's coding.

W3C.org also has processes to check whether all the links on your site are active. While this is important for SEO, it is also important in creating a great user experience. Remove all dead links because a site with broken links gives the impression that your information is out of date.

As mentioned earlier, it is important that you do not have your entire site in Flash. Although Flash sites are generally more impressive to users and it's true that there are ways to track activity on Flash sites, search engines still *cannot* read Flash files or image files. If you decide to use a Flash site, then most of your ranking will come from your URL, page title, and linking text to your site. This misses out on many other helpful ways of getting your site ranked—namely content.

External Components:

OFF-SITE INTEGRATION

The SEO strategies we've discussed so far have been items that are, more or less, in your control. Now we'll spend some time looking at external components that can boost your search engine rankings; these external components are more dependent on others' support of your site. Even so, there are still things you can do to leverage your site and content.

The key goal of this stage is to do all you can to generate incoming links to your site. It is better to have a few incoming links from relevant and quality sites than to have lots more incoming links from "no name" sites. To give you an idea of your starting point, search Yahoo! for "link:www.yoursite.org." This search will show you who are linking to your site. By this you can determine how many links are coming to your site, where they are coming from, and whether they are from relevant sites.

Yahoo! Site Explorer offers the most comprehensive list of backlinks for any website and gives you the option of exporting the backlink list into a more readable list.

WHAT IS PAGERANK?

PageRank is a number Google uses as a part of their formula for determining quality sites. Some of the determinants that go into this number are the traffic to a site, how often the site is updated, the quality of coding on the site, and the number of links to the site from pages with a high PageRank.[6] The PageRank can be from 0 – 9; a higher number is better.

Not only do you want your site to have a high PageRank, but you also want sites with high PageRank to link *to* your site.

As you grow in your understanding of search engine marketing, you will come across PageRank often. Do not focus on this too much. While it can be an ego boost to have high PageRank, if you are not focusing on relevant keywords, high PageRank will not help you get new traffic to your site.

SO HOW DO YOU GET LINKS TO YOUR SITE?

The easiest and most harmful method for generating incoming links is to use a link broker. Companies abound promising to get you links from quality sites (i.e. high PageRank, government and education sites, directories). It would be best for you to ignore them. Some might work for you, but in general these service providers are attempting to subvert the system. They may give you a short-term solution, but you run the risk of getting blacklisted by Google or entering into a regular subscription fee service. One of the best benefits of SEO is the residual effects of increasing free traffic to your site. When you use link brokers, you face the potential of losing all your efforts through blacklisting or the possibility of long term subscription fees to maintain the level of traffic the link brokers produced for you.

An alternative to buying links is to go with directory sites. Most directory sites will charge an annual fee, but for ministries the only directory that will be necessary to buy into would be Yahoo!

6   For more information go to Google's write up on PageRank: (*http://www.google.com/corporate/tech.html*).

Remember that Yahoo! began as a cataloger of websites and is given weight in most search engine calculations. You can submit your site under the city and state in which your ministry is located and that alone will help your site to come up in local searches. Other useful directories are DMOZ, state and national denomination directories, local business directories, local Chambers of Commerce, Yellow Pages and Google Maps.

Google Maps is a great place for you to position your site. Not only does this site help people get directions to your ministry, but it can become a vital source of advertising. You can use the map to give the exact location of your ministry. You can also add pictures of the building, services or events. You can also leave ministry times, contact information and a link to your ministry's website. Google Maps seems to draw information from SuperPages.com which is another free service to which you can submit your information.

A quick search on Google Maps for churches in Madison, MS comes up with Ridgecrest Baptist. They have added pictures to their listing, so searchers can see aspects of their church. They have also included the church's webpage and contact email. This allows someone new to Madison to quickly find relevant information about Ridgecrest Baptist. This person may even be more inclined to visit Ridgecrest because finding the information was such a seamless experience.

LINKS FROM PERSONAL CONTACTS

Your base of potential links to your site is as big as your network of contacts. You can get incoming links from colleagues, friends, traveling speakers, missionaries, staff, staff's friends, etc. If you have someone speak at your ministry, have them link their site to yours. You can also link back to theirs as you announce them coming or talk about what they shared. People within your ministry can link to your webpages from personal websites or blogs. Committed members will love to do this simple task to help the ministry's growth. The key here is to use text links, not banners. Banners are prettier, but they are not considered links to your site.

> *Social networking sites, such as Facebook, Flickr, Twitter, and MySpace, have a no-follow tag on their links. These links will still be good for exposure, but will not help in search engine ranking.*

By way of example, let me share this brief story with you. Lowe's Home Improvement created a campaign to leverage their partnership with real estate agents by giving them banners to put on their individual sites to link to the Lowe's moving site. These banners began to pop up on thousands of agents' sites and started to send referral traffic. Because most of these Realtors did not include a text link to the moving site, this campaign to boost search ranking never gained momentum for Lowe's.

You can post instructions on your site for how you would like people to link to you. This will provide your partners with direction on what would be helpful to you as they give to your ministry in a very simple way. The instructions can also help you provide targeted keywords to your partners. Keywords in text links are weighted heavily with search engines in determining search engine rankings.

Another linking strategy is to share links with local missions groups with which you're already partnered. If the partnership is anything newsworthy, you should send a press release to your local newspaper. You can also send similar press releases to denominational magazines and Christian blogs. Remember to include your website on any press release to gain that quality link.[7]

ADDITIONAL LINK SITES

LinkedIn.com: LinkedIn is an online business networking tool. People use LinkedIn to keep up with where friends and former

---

7 For additional information on how to write and submit a press release, go to: http://www.prwebdirect.com/pressreleasetips.php.

colleagues are now working and to make referrals and introductions for new potential employers, employees and other business connections. Have your entire staff sign up for LinkedIn accounts; setting up an account is easy and can be done in a matter of a few minutes.

The benefit of LinkedIn is to get ranking for each staff's name and to create relevant links to your site. LinkedIn allows you to set up three website links. If you select the category "Other," you can type in the description you want to use for the link. This way you can get a quality link to your site with a desired keyword phrase (e.g. City, State: Ministry Name). You can use the other two links to go to your blog or community events.

Flickr: Opening a Flickr account is a perfect way to have a ministry photo site. It does not flow as well as if it was on your site, but the search benefits will greatly outweigh that. Setting up the site is not difficult. Once you create an account, edit the profile to get your ministry name in the URL and create a link back to your ministry's website. Some basic HTML coding will be necessary: <a href="http://www.yoursite.org">City, State: Ministry Name </a>.

Here are additional benefits to using this site:

- Most people are familiar with the format.
- They can search within Flickr to find you, and this will go to other search engines and image searches.
- You can and should create relevant alt tags for each picture.
- Each picture allows you to create some HTML code in the description, which can link back to your site.
- You can also create tags for the pictures to group by special events, dates, ministries, members and more for ease of browsing.

These links are no longer added into search rankings, but the images on this site still get viewed and these links are followed by people who see the images. I created a blog and posted all images for the blog on Flickr instead of on the actual blog. This led to additional traffic to the blog from people who found those images on Flickr.

Blogger & WordPress: When you're ready to start blogging, using a blog tool like Blogger or WordPress for your blog service keeps you from having to reinvent the wheel. The other great benefit is that you can build on the PageRank that these services already have. Both of these services allow for you to "plug" them into your site, which allows a better experience for your site's visitors. Your web designer should be able to create a matching template of your site for the blog interface.

The main thing to remember with setting up a blog is not to start if you are not going to commit to continue. For an individual this is not a big deal, but it leaves a negative impression for a ministry's blog to have a two-month-old post as its most recent entry.

Pulling it all together

Search engine optimization (SEO) can be summed up in three categories of work:

1. Keyword Analysis
2. On-Site Integration
3. Off-Site Optimization

Focusing on these three categories will help you keep your hands around SEO. This is the science behind all that it will take to get your website ranked. To get everything you can out of SEO, the rest is art. In fact, the rest of this book is looking at specific ways to judge how you are doing or ways to improve this backbone of SEO. If you start to have questions as we move forward, come back to this chapter to help explain the basics—the science behind the art.

Chapter 3

The Measure of Success

Don't Let This Happen to You

HomeDepotMoving.com is a site that the Home Depot uses to attract people who are in the process of buying a home, selling a home and/or moving from one location to another. People in this stage of life are highly attractive customers because according to some estimates their annual spend is 7x the amount of the average home owner. A partnership with the USPS change of address had always brought a lot of traffic to their site, so when that partnership was not renewed for 2008, they endeavored to refresh the site.

They launched a brand-new redesign with a great user experience. The content was well laid out, and the imagery was just beautiful. Unfortunately, they built the site completely with Flash.

If you've been reading along since page 1 of this book, you know by now that search engines had no way of determining what was on the Flash-based site. Remember that search engines read the code of your site; they cannot read images, videos or Flash. The image on the next page shows how Google saw their website:

Live View of HomeDepotMoving.com

(accessed 02/24/2008)

Text-Only View of HomeDepotMoving.com

(accessed 02/24/2008)

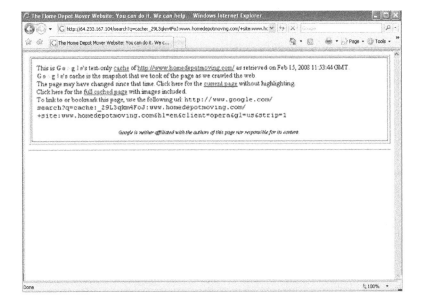

In one fatal swoop, the Home Depot Moving site lost all organic traffic. To make matters worse, they changed the navigation on the site, so all the rankings they previously had for other pages on their site were lost. Why? They changed the URLs without leaving a trail for search engines to find the new locations.

Google's Index of HomeDepotMoving.com pages

(accessed 02/19/2008)

At the time of this writing, I am unsure how long it will take Home Depot to figure out what went wrong. They no doubt use tracking software, but they expected losing traffic with the loss of the USPS partnership—so maybe they'll never fully "connect the dots" as to why traffic dipped so dramatically with their website redesign. This is just one reason why tracking is so important; by spotting errors quickly, you can fix whatever is broken right away and minimize any negative impact on your traffic.

> *If you are currently not tracking your web traffic, immediately go to Google Analytics (www.google.com/analytics/) and register your site. You can never really determine the success of your site without knowing the data.*
>
> *Most web analytic programs are roughly the same. The privileges of the paid programs are the charts and large data storage. Google Analytics is free and its storage is enough to cover a large retailer like Home Depot. All my examples and discussion will be based on what can be done with this service.*

I've got the data, but what am I looking at?

If you have Google Analytics, then you have a great deal of information at your fingertips—but all that data can be overwhelming if you do not know what you are looking at. Even though you get preset charts and data, they are still meaningless without context. Let's start by assigning meaning to the feel good numbers.

What everyone wants to know is: "How many people are coming to my site?" To answer this question, let's learn about two metrics (most people use them interchangeably): visits and unique visitors. Unfortunately these metrics are not interchangeable numbers; they are just used that way. The second most popular question is: "What pages are people reading? In web tracking terminology, this is known as pageviews.

If you are looking for how many *people* have visited your site, then you need to look at the unique visitors' statistic. If you are looking for how many *times* your site has been visited, then you need visits. The visits statistic takes into account when people return to your site. To explain this more accurately, visits are the number of sessions that someone has been browsing your site. If they leave and come back, this starts a new session and counts as a new visit. Pageviews are simply the number of pages people have accessed on your site.

Metric	Pros	Cons
Visits	Number of times site accessed	Which are new / returning visitors?
Unique Visits	Number of people who come to site	How long do you wait until you recount returning visitors?
Page views	Number of pages accessed	Is this large because people cannot find what they want?

These statistics are always the most popular because they make the site owner happy or sad depending on the size of the numbers. A lot of visits equal celebration, but what does that really tell you?

One of the best analyses you can perform with this data is to plot the daily stats over a year. The spikes or valleys tell you whether or not different campaigns drove people to the site, or what times of year people are likely to be on your site. Summertime is generally a low attendance time for churches, so is your congregation listening to your sermons online or are they going to other resources to keep connected? Or looking at week-by-week trends, do you see a spike on Mondays as people follow-up on what they learned on Sunday?

Personally, I feel these numbers are best when looked at over a period of time. Then you can identify changes in the numbers and open up to good questions. Have recent changes to your site made an impact on visits? The numbers by themselves are useless; you need to discover the story they are telling.

When you start really getting into the web analytics, there are two main areas to focus on: navigation on the site and navigation to the site.

Navigation on the Site

Navigation on the site tells you how well laid out your site is. Are people able to navigate with ease? Are they led to the pages you want them to see? What are the most popular pages? What types of content are people drawn to? How can you leverage what is already working? How can you fix what is not?

Let's say that you have a singles ministry at your church. You think it is great, and it has a nicely laid out section on your church's website. To determine its success, look at the top content section of Google Analytics. This area shows you which pages people are going to on your site. Where does the singles page rank for your content? If it is not a high percentage of those who visit your site, then you realize you might have a problem to address. Maybe the singles ministry is not that great, maybe the page is difficult to find, or maybe it's not a huge need in your city. Whatever the case, knowing the data sets you in motion to find out what solution is needed.

Another useful tool is the depth of visit. I personally feel the depth of visit statistic is better than the pageviews. Web analysts commonly divide the pageviews by visits and say that the average visitor looks at something like 3.7 pages. But that is not true. What if the average visitor to your site is only looking at the homepage then leaving?

The depth of visit statistic will show how many people only looked at one page, which you can then use to calculate how many pages everyone else is viewing.

Another basic metric for navigation on the site is top content. This is important because it tells you what the majority of visitors are looking at. You can look at this by URL or by Page Title. I would suggest you make sure that each page has its own separate, distinctive page title, and then use the Page Title function. Although there are fixes for the advanced, the URL ranking will count capitals as a separate URL (e.g. UBC.org and ubc.org will be listed separately).

The top content will show you what people are looking at on your site. Are your sermons frequently visited? Are new visitors to the site looking at the staff or ministries? Are people coming to view the church calendar? These things are helpful to know and can give you hints as to what might need refreshing, what might need not to exist or what is just difficult to find.

As an example of something that's hard to find, a family member recently sent me a slideshow on one of the online photo sites. This person had taken some nice pictures of my kids of which I wanted to get copies. At first it seemed that the site did not allow for downloads of the pictures but finally, after some poking around, I found a link on the bottom right that allowed for what I was trying to do. Does your site have a resource that people would like but cannot find easily?

Navigation to the Site

Navigation to the site tells you how people are finding your site. This gives you a wealth of information about how you are doing. There are four main channels people use to access a site: direct, referral, organic or banners. A faithful review of how people are getting to your site will help you to know how to proceed in getting in front of more people.

Direct Traffic: Direct traffic is people either typing in your web URL or referencing a bookmark to your site from their web browser. The main way to differentiate between the two is to determine if the visitor to the site is new or returning. A new visitor will not have bookmarked your site; they would have typed it in. These people have more than likely seen your advertising somewhere or they may have recently visited your church and left with a bulletin. It is possible they guessed your URL if you were able to secure something relevant for your church (e.g. Spencer United Methodist Church is SpencerUMC.org).

Direct traffic will consist of your most engaged visitors. They already know who you are, and they are coming to your site for a specific reason. Maybe they thought you had a really good resource that they are coming back for, maybe they forgot your service times, or maybe they are coming to read the pastor's blog. These answers are a little harder to find. You can go to direct traffic and look at landing page, but the majority of this will be the homepage because it is usually easier to remember or type in. What you can do is go to the top content report and pick some of the suspected pages. Then from there you can pull down the breakdown by source. It is a roundabout way, but it will give you an idea of where people are going.

Referral Traffic: Referral traffic is someone linking to your site. These are the nice sites that think you have something worth sharing and have pointed people to your website. As mentioned earlier, this is a big metric in how search engines place your ranking in their results. This is also important because it shows who is being successful in directing people to your site.

You can improve your site's rank by thinking through relevant links to you. Does your denomination's website have a link to you? Are people finding you from them? Do you have people involved with your ministry that have websites that can link to you? Are there any other ministries you work with that point people to you? Look through the referral traffic report and see who is pointing people to you. Are there any similar people you can ask to link to you?

When you look through the report, you can find additional information by investigating the site that is linking to you. What are they saying about you? If they are saying wonderful things, write a comment on their website acknowledging their kind words. If what they have to say is negative, this may be an opportunity to reach out to them to share your perspective or just open up a loving dialog. This has the effect of negating the potential damage their write-up about you is saying and gives you an opportunity to frame the discussion around yourself.

One great example I saw about this was in 2007. Willow Creek came out with a statement about their ministry which many took as a departure from how they had done ministry for years. Christianity Today posted an article on their Out of Ur blog stating, "Willow Creek Repents?[8]" The article gave the impression of a complete turnaround at Willow Creek, and it started a feverish response in comments which lasted for eight days until Greg Hawkins of Willow Creek entered into the discussion to clarify what had actually been said. Christianity Today then turned off the comments to make the statement from Willow Creek easy to find.

What had happened was people who for whatever reason had issues with Willow Creek took the article as an opportunity to express their differences and make it seem that Willow Creek finally came to see how wrong they were. Hawkins statement brought the discussion to an end and reduced ongoing negative comments through this blog.

Organic Traffic: Organic traffic is comprised of people who find your site from searches online. A brief view of this is important to make sure you are indexed on all the main search engines. Click on the search engines listed to see what keywords people are using to

---

8 Scaramanga, Url. "Willow Creek Repents?" Out Ur Blog. October 18, 2007. http://blog.christianitytoday.com/outofur/archives/2007/10/willow_creek_re.html accessed 9/12/2009.

finding you. If there are keywords that you feel you should be listed for that are not listed, then you have identified an area that you can improve on your site. Remember that Google Analytics will give you more information than you need, so determining which battles to fight will be important to your success.

You can also get to keywords directly. This is a better place to go to check specific keywords irrespective of which search engine was used. The keywords can also be divided between paid and non-paid links.

Paid links are the top and right hand results on search engines. These companies paid the search engines to have their sites ranked in those positions. It does not help with your natural search rankings, but it can be a great tool to decide the best keywords for you to go after. By setting up paid searches, you can try out different keywords to go after, and measure the success rate of the traffic it produces. Do these visitors to your site do what you want them to do? You only pay for the traffic that comes through these search terms. Therefore you can tell whether people are actually searching for certain terms before you update content on your site for those terms. You can also test the title and description that will go with the paid result. Once you find a keyword that works, then you create content for your site that goes after that keyword. You then transfer the paid search term with organic results by what you update on your site.

If you are deciding between paid search and banner ads, I would suggest paid search. Paid search is cheaper; you only pay for visits to your site; and you come away with actual data. Banner ads are priced by impressions, which you cannot measure and on which you may not capitalize.

Campaign Traffic: Campaign traffic is made of people who come to your site through links that you paid for. These people may have found you through banner ads, purchased links or any link on which you create a campaign URL.

Banner ads are the images placed on websites that direct visitors to go to another site. Much of the content on the web is supported by these banners. The purpose of these banners is to get exposure on the web where your target customer will see it. Therefore many banners are animated to draw your eye to the banner. Successful banner ads need to communicate the reason to go to your site in 5-10 seconds. It is not a place to use a lot of words, but it is a place you will frequently see the word "Free."

Banner ads have no benefit for search. The links are generally ignored by search engines. You might drive incremental traffic as long as you pay for the banner, but as soon as the banner comes down, the extra traffic will leave.

Purchased links are designed to get relevant links to your site. You will frequently see links to purchase on .edu sites, specialized directories or blogs. The goal of purchased links is to get yourself on sites that have high page rank, within your field, using specified keywords in the link. These can be great links for search, but if they're caught as paid links, then your site can theoretically be penalized. From what I can tell, those penalized are really limited to high profile SEO marketers who are promoting the practice, and the search engine programmers decide to make a example out of them. This practice is not illegal; it's just that the programmers of the search algorithms desire to keep the field of search engine optimization pure.

Most paid advertising is tagged within the URL so that Google Analytics can pull the referral links into a campaign section. The traffic from campaigns will be broken out however you designate the URL.[9] The benefit from this is to quickly determine the benefits from these paid traffic sources.

---

9   Google has a site that will help you with developing these tracking URL's. (http://www.google.com/support/googleanalytics/bin/answer.py?answer=55578&hl=en)

The main items included in the tracking URLs are: source, medium, term, content and name.

- Source   – What site the banner is located
- Medium   – Location of the banner: side banner, run of site, email, paid search, etc.
- Term   – Keywords: mainly for paid search
- Content   – Banner size, type, or reason for location
- Name   – Reason for this banner

> *There are many URL shorteners on the web now that can take a long URL and make it short. Therefore if you use Twitter or Facebook for your ministry, any links to back to your site should use tracking URLs that have been shortened. The one exception is if you are trying to brand your homepage URL. These links do not add to search but you can track them, and the data will be helpful to you. You can also use the shortened URLs on emails to track the effectiveness of those as well.*

Final Words on Studying the Data

Measuring the success of your website is probably the most important thing you can do in order to get people on the site. Are you leveraging this asset to the full measure of its potential? We are commanded to make the most of every opportunity, yet we limit this command to only our spiritual life. We serve a God that is sovereign over everything; therefore, we are responsible with all He has entrusted to us.

Data can be very confusing at first, especially to those who are not mathematically inclined. Even so, as Spirit-filled Christians we can do all things in Christ who strengthens us. Our minds are not limited to just our natural abilities and strengths. For whatsoever is beneficial, we have all we need to do it with practice and the supernatural help of the Holy Spirit.

Do not be discouraged. Just as many of you ask for the Spirit's help to enlighten the Scriptures, He will gladly help those who ask of Him to get your site visible to those who need to see it.

With this said, your website's web data will differ from the data of other ministry websites. Your site serves a specific purpose for your ministry, and the measures of success will be dependent on the purpose you have created. This will be the topic of the next chapter.

Chapter 4

Why Do You Have a Website?

Do you even need a website?

This is often the most overlooked question when most ministries are beginning planning their online presence. I tend to believe every ministry needs a website, yet most ministries' websites are ineffective because they never thought through this question. Without vision, nations fail. Without a driving purpose, websites tend to be cheap DIY sites or expensive Flash playgrounds—neither of which will likely produce the desired results.

You cannot fully answer the question about your need for a website without first answering these two questions:

1. Why does your ministry exist?
2. What are the measures of success for your ministry?

These questions really need to be answered in prayer, and if you have not considered these questions, I would strongly encourage ministry leaders to think through these two questions right away.

Case Study:

CAMPUS CRUSADE FOR CHRIST

Let's consider Campus Crusade for Christ. The reason the ministry started was: "To turn lost students into Christ-centered laborers." The stated goal is clear, concise and measureable. Campus Crusade had two overarching metrics to determine success: (1.) Conversions, and (2.) New Staff. The direction they gave to meet their vision statement was: "To win, build, send." This added new metrics: Numbers of students involved in Bible studies, attending conferences and going on summer mission trips. Crusade recently added this new direction: "To build movements everywhere," which adds the number of movements to the metrics.

Ultimately, Jesus alone determines the success of your ministry, but these metrics are great tools to gauge what you are actually accomplishing. From this vantage point you are able to determine the strategy you need to move forward with Internet-based support for your ministry. Let's continue with Campus Crusade.

Crusade is large enough that they need a multi-site strategy as they approach the Internet. As conversions are strategic in their ministry, they need sites that address reaching non-Christians and moving them toward the love of Christ. The data these sites would consider as important are the number of new visitors if it is a simple Gospel presentation site, or the number of returning visitors if it is a site designed for on-going dialogue.

Their sites direct visitors to a decision, and give users an opportunity to indicate whether they are a new believer. A Crusade staff member can then follow-up with the new believer and the site manager can determine whether the website is meeting its stated purpose. These sites need to rank highly on the search engines. Someone doing a search on "Who is Jesus?" could be highly likely to receive Christ. Therefore looking at the navigation to the site will also be of great interest to Crusade.

Crusade also needs conference and summer missions websites. Conversion rates will be a great metric for these sites. How many people who come to the site request an application? If the conversion rate is low, then site managers need to consider if the application is difficult to find. There should also be a large number of referring links to these sites from each of the local ministries' websites, which can tell you which local ministry is engaged.

For Campus Crusade, the last type of site we'll consider is a site to help create movements. With this new initiative, there should be an informational site to help local ministries start these new movements. There should be resources like definitions, suggestions, Bible studies, marketing material, etc. This would be a great site for a blog or a discussion group. This site should be the "information expert" on movement building. Therefore it should rank highly for the following keywords: "small group ministry," "growth groups," "leading a Bible study," etc.

Can you see how each of these sites serves different purposes, but each drive the success of the overall goals of the ministry? The first site will target people who are not Christians while the last site will target those who are. They will also be looking at different metrics of success. If they create a nice evangelical site and get a ton of visitors, is it successful? You don't know. Are all of the visitors coming from Orlando (Crusade's headquarters)? Is all the traffic coming from referral links? What types of sites are referring to it? Do these sites typically attract non-Christians? Are people indicating decisions for Christ? You might come to the conclusion that the new cool site is getting traffic from Christians who think it is fun, but also conclude that non-Christians don't know it exists.

Types of Websites

Once you have determined your ministry's purpose, you can determine what you would like to accomplish with your website. There are basically six major types of websites that you want to think through. Each accomplishes different goals; you can mix and match the different genres to best suit the needs and goals of your ministry. The six types of websites are:

- Web Advertisement
- Extended Brochure
- Resource Library
- Soapbox Site
- E-commerce
- Online Community

Static Pages: Web advertisement sites and extended brochure sites are generally static pages. Static page websites are set-up once and are only infrequently updated with minor maintenance. These are great for ministries that know that they will not take the time and effort to maintain the sites. This is a better choice than creating a site that claims to be up-to-date, but was last updated months ago.

Web Advertisement: A web advertisement site is simply an extension to your other advertisements. It is a simple one-page site that explains your ministry, what needs you meet and provides your contact information. This is the bare minimum of an online presence. Owners of only these sites are probably not reading this book, but you might have pages on your site that work as such. If you think of each page as a type of site, you might have many pages that function as web advertisements. This type of site can be put up quickly and used as a placeholder until your complete a more thorough online plan.

Extended Brochure: An extended brochure site is an amplified web advertisement. These sites will take portions of your ministry and create separate pages for each part. Generally these sites are a collection of web advertisements for you ministry. The home page will function as a menu, serving up what is inside the website. You can have a staff page, services page, contact page, etc. This type of site allows people to investigate your ministry more.

Neither of these two sites is directed toward returning visitors, but people investigating your ministry for the first time. Neither of these sites will generate much traffic, so if you are thinking about going this route, you should not invest much money. You will still want these sites to look professional as they will create an impression of your ministry, but it will be hard to justify a large expenditure.

Incremental Pages: Incremental pages are pages that index an ever-increasing amount of reference material. There is always something new to read; as such, a properly managed incremental page can become a "go- to" location for your niche. Incremental pages are great because they add new content to your site, which works to improve your search rankings. It is important that you continue to add information to these types of sites, otherwise they will become as irrelevant as a newspaper that arrives two months late.

Resource Library: A resource library is a collection of resources that is beneficial to your specific niche. What type of information would be of interest to your target audience? Is this unique information you can create or are their already places online to which you can link? These sites can be a collection of articles, videos, sermons, pictures, etc.

This type of site will need to be updated regularly to stay relevant to your audience. Adding a resource library to your church or ministry website can encourage repeat-traffic to your site and increase your search engine ranking. It also improves the trust for your ministry as knowledgeable in the field you are working. You, as the site author, have the added benefit of continuing to improve your knowledge base as you research information to add to this type of site.

Soapbox Site: A soapbox site is slightly different than a resource library in that instead of providing relevant resources, this type is your interpretation of information within your segment of influence. These sites are typically blogs, but they can also be a collection of articles. Some ministry leaders tend to this type of site because they enjoy stirring things up. This type of site works well when complemented with ways for visitors to comment on the information online.

As I mentioned earlier in this book, I encourage pastors to consider creating—and maintaining!—blogs. This type of site allows people a window into the leader of the ministry and creates a face for the ministry. Someone looking for a new church will learn a lot about a ministry by looking at a pastor's blog, since it is the pastor who has the most face-time at a church. If someone likes the pastor's blog, then they will more than likely like the church.

Interactive Pages: Interactive pages are webpages that are asking something from the visitors to the site. It could request the visitor to purchase something or to create an on-going dialog. These are more difficult to pull off but, if done well, they can create a nice benefit for your ministry.

E-commerce: E-commerce sites provide resources to purchase. If you are going to collect money online, you will need to make sure your site is very secure. This book will not go into the details of e-commerce security except to say that you must make sure your site is under a SSL certificate for the protection of you and your customers.

This type of site can be risky because you are saying that you have something that people will be willing to purchase. Sermons are commonly available for purchase. Because of the abundance of sermons available online for free, you are making a statement that you have something that is said differently and has greater value. There are pastors out there who can do this. Are you one of them? In short, if you're going to sell something online, make sure that you have prayed through that decision. Should the information be free to all? By making someone pay for it, does it give a greater sense of value to your product? Is this income more important than the reduction of potential users of the product? The main thing I would suggest is that you check your motives.

Online Community: An online community is a gathering place of people with similar interests. It's a place where people can discuss topics, share things they like and keep in touch. These types of pages can be discussion groups, social networks and collaborative work (wiki) sites.

Community sites are hard to get off the ground because they take a decent-sized following to develop the momentum for people to add content. But, if you were to succeed in getting your community site off the ground, the quantity of new material and the traffic to your site would definitely improve to your search rankings.

Typical Sections of Ministry Websites

Once you have determined which type of site you will go with, what do you need to put on the site? Part of the answer to this question depends on the type you go with, but there is specific information you must consider if you are going to be effective online. Here're the basics:

Name: Who Are You? Don't try to hide who you are. Say you decide to create an evangelical website where you want to get people thinking about the claims of Christ. You think that people will be cautious of reaching out to you if they think you are a church. Even if you are right, being obscure and secretive gives the impression that you are not trustworthy or not sure of what you are selling. Be up front with who you are. Take responsibility for the content you put on the web.

Whatever site your ministry starts should have the name of your ministry on the footer of every page. If this is your main site, you should also have your name on every page's title bar. This allows people to quickly find out who is authoring the content.

Purpose: What Do You Want? This also falls into the same category as not hiding who you are. If someone is looking around for a church, they should easily find what your church is all about and what makes you different. They are thinking, "If I join this church, what do they what out of me?" More than likely you want them to fall more in love with Jesus or become a better Christian in some way. How does your church go about this? Make this easy to find.

Typically websites have an "about us" section for this information, but whatever you are really about—your main purpose—this will be all over your website. If you main thing is the Bible, then you will put it in your name and/or catch phrase. You will talk about how your pastors have exegetical sermons. You will funnel people to your Bible study classes. And, Scripture verses will be all over your site. The same would be if your church's focus was missions. You would have pictures from your church's previous mission trips. You would highlight how you prioritize missions giving. And, you would funnel people to the prayer room so they could pray for your missionaries.

Letting people know why you exist and what you want from them allows them to relax on your site. They know what you want, so they are not wondering where the bait and switch will take place. For example, this church is all about the Bible, so I should be able to get some good Bible resources from it. Or, that ministry is all about helping the poor, so I can find some connections to help my church's cell group volunteer for a local ministry.

Contact: How Can You Be Reached? Let's take the previous example of the cell group looking for a local ministry with which to get involved. They are on your site and find a couple of ministries that interest them. What are they to do next? If there is not a way to contact you, it's like a book that addresses your felt need in the first few chapters, but does not address what you are to do in the end. You are left feeling more frustrated than when you started. I want to participate in this church, but I cannot find how to start this involvement.

You should always have some form of contact. If you have a physical location, have clear directions, a phone number and hours of operation. If you are just providing an online service, make sure you have an email address so that people can ask questions, and possibly a phone number to talk to a live person.

More than likely, you will need a website for your ministry, but not just any website will work the best. It is not true that if you build it they will come. It is not even true that if you build it *well* they will come. Take these questions to the Lord and think through what will be best for your ministry.

Chapter 5

Do You Need a Blog?

What's the Point?

More than likely, if you lead a ministry or a subsection of a ministry, then you feel a special calling from the Lord to do what you are doing. Therefore, God is working in you regarding what He wants to get across to the people He has brought your way.

Writing a blog is a great way to get your thoughts down "on paper" and help you process them. It allows those in your ministry to see what is going on in your life and in your mind. You get to share what impassions you. It can be fodder for sermons. You can clarify on what you have said earlier or on what you have seen. You can also get feedback from others, so you can better identify where they are coming from.

Blogging to Improve Your Search Results

Beyond the benefits outlined above, blogging has other benefits. A blog allows you to enhance your web presence by adding new and fresh content to your site regularly. Remember that content is king when it comes to getting ranked by search engines. So, with every article you write and comment you gather, your site has a better chance to come up in an organic search. As you move forward with writing a blog, consider the following four areas: The blog title, the blog subject, the blog comments and the maintenance.

Blog Title: By blog title I mean the title for each entry you write. The title is the first thing people see and by this they determine whether or not the article will be interesting enough to read. Just as the titles of your webpages are important, so are the titles to each blog entry. These are the words that have high importance on search and the first impressions people get from search results.

When thinking through the blog title, second to figuring out what the entry is about you should determine what is the best phrase to pick up search traffic. What words or phrases is your target audience searching for? Does the title make a compelling reason for people to read your blog entry?

Blog Subject: The best way to optimize the content for your blog is to create a content schedule. Make a list of all the topics that would be of interest to your target audience and keep a record of when you address those topics. This will allow you to remain well-rounded and attract a larger net of your target. Your content schedule should also consider keywords you want to target for search optimization. Although search should not guide your blog, it will be beneficial to keep it in mind.

Subjects for your blog entries should also come from recent news and other bloggers' posts. Five benefits you receive from this are:

1. Maintaining relevance for your blog
2. Increasing your industry knowledge
3. Developing networking relationships with other bloggers
4. Adding incoming links and traffic to your blog
5. Strengthening your role as a thought leader

Also, recent news is going to receive a short-term boost in searches. Getting in early can get you a quick burst of traffic to your blog.

Blog Comments: Encourage comments and read/respond to comments that people make on your blog. This is a unique benefit that blogs have over ordinary websites; blogs are special because they encourage interaction with site visitors. Comments on your blog are a sign to new visitors that you have engaging content. Ending a blog post with a question encourages comments. Taking a quick survey also gets people engaged (i.e. they will come back to the site to find out what others have said).

Replying to comments encourages comments. It signals to the visitors of your blog that you read the comments, and that they can expect an answer to questions they may pose. You can develop relationships and further discussion with visitors, and you can grow in your understanding as you get feedback and are sometimes challenged by those who post comments and ask questions.

Blog Maintenance: Promote what you write. You can have great content and use optimized keywords, but links to the blog will generate the momentum to your site and increase your search rankings. Utilizing simple online tools can help you generate these links. First, your blog platform should promote RSS feeds, trackbacks and social bookmarks. Second, you need to actively get your name out there by commenting on other blogs and adding your site to blog directories.

RSS Feeds: This is a tool that allows people to pull your content onto their site. This rarely helps your search ranking, but it does provide an easy way for others to read new posts on your site. Most people online are following several blogs, and RSS feeds allow them to pull all the blogs into one source, cutting down the time it would take to go to each blog.

Feedburner is a get resource for setting up RSS feeds. It is also great because you can then track the number of people using the tool to pull your content. This is easy to set up. Once you've set up RSS feeds, promote them on your site.

Trackbacks: This is a tool that shows you who has referenced your post on their blog. This is a way to show someone that you like what they have written, and others can see the amount of interest your post has generated. This does seem to have a positive effect on search as it tells the search engines that someone likes your post.

Social Bookmarks: This is a tool where people vote on your post. Digg, StumbleUpon, Technorati, Facebook, and Twitter are all tools that allow your blog to be shared with others. The Internet has many collections of social groups, and by making it easy for people to share your post with their friends, you will greatly expand your influence.

Commenting on Other Blogs: Writing relevant comments on others' blogs creates goodwill for you to other blog influencers. This encourages these bloggers to pay attention to your blog and then potentially send readers to your blog. It is good to find other people who are in the same field you are in but another market. It is a form of networking, but it also adds value to your blog. Commenting on some blogs adds what Internet marketers call "link love" or "link juice" to your blog. This is not true on every blog, but most bloggers do pay attention to those people's blogs who leave good comments on their blog.

Blog Directories: This works the same as directories to which you would add your site except these are directories just for blogs. Refer to chapter 2 for more on directories.

What Blog Platform should I use?

For the most part, it does not matter what blog platform you use. Some web hosting services provide a blog platform for you. There are also free services such as WordPress and Blogger that are easy to integrate into your site. The main thing you should remember is to make sure you use your own domain name. You lose a lot of search juice by using the standard URL (i.e. yourblog.blogspot.com or yourblog.wordpress.com).

Start Blogging Today

The main thing is to start blogging. New content in a search engine's mind equals a relevant site. A blog with regular posts brings the search engines back more often to scan your site in order to index the new content. And, on top of everything else, the more you write, the more you grow personally, pushing you to learn your topics more in depth.

Read other people's blogs. See what is relevant and what the common trends are in your field. This will help spur ideas on what to write about and will help you know with whom to build relationships. This will be beneficial for you and those in your ministry as you broaden what you know. Reading blogs is as much a determinant of a well-read person as reading trade magazines and newspapers.

Comment on what you are learning. By discussing a book you have read or referencing another person's blog, you are resourcing your readers to information that may be beneficial for them to check out. As a ministry leader, you desire to give people whatever you can to help them grow.

Blogging is as great a way to disperse information as giving a sermon each week. Your readers can take in morsels of thought and chew them over. You can provide links that they can check out immediately. Blogging can take time, but by dedicating a portion of time each week to this task, you can add an additional resource to supplement your ministry.

Chapter 6

Are Emails Effective?

The potential of Email Newsletters

Are emails effective? The question almost sounds silly. People have been moving to email for years now. Postage rates are continually going up; it is almost an easy decision to go free over almost $0.50. Even so, the question is still valid.

Everybody has email. Most people even have multiple addresses. What is so hard about this form of communication? Surprisingly, a lot. First of all, spam filters and junk folders block many companies' emails. Second, sending out blanket emails without permission could anger recipients and send more of your emails to spam filters. Third, most people are using email for work and the thought of adding more time to email is rather dreary. Still, the downfalls of email are mainly technique. Later in this chapter, I will go over some helpful things to think through before sending out an email.

The advantages of email are tremendous when done well, but they are most beneficial when they are planned out. An email can get immediate satisfaction; it can elicit feedback; it can lead people where you want them to go online; and it is easily trackable. But over and above these reasons, email newsletters keep people engaged with you.

Immediate Communication: This is a positive and negative for emails. If you need to get some news out quickly, as an urgent prayer request, there is nothing much quicker than email. And yet, you have to be careful because not everything is urgent. Once everything becomes urgent the response rate drops quickly.

The ease of email also makes the communication immediate. You can throw together a quick note to a distribution list in a matter of seconds. Again, because of the ease, you might also easily send mistakes to everyone on your list. For instance, you want to send an urgent email out regarding a fund-raising dinner. In your haste you enter the wrong time or wrong date. In one quick act you just lowered the number of people attending because they are now confused about when it is being held. Even if you catch your mistake and send out yet another email, the confusion has already been created and some damage done.

Immediacy is a great tool, but it must be handled with care. Proofread all emails going out. Have a very detailed person proof all email blasts, get an approval process and question yourself about whether an email is necessary. Simple steps to slow down can reduce carelessness and maintain trust from those on your email list.

Elicit Feedback: If your ministry ever needs feedback from people, email is one of the best means. This is especially true if you are looking for detailed information. The results will already be in digital form which makes it easier to process. And, people have the opportunity to fill it out at their convenience.

Email usually sits in someone's inbox until they respond. Therefore if you are looking for feedback it would be a constant reminder in their inbox until they make time to give you the response. A follow-up email after a short interval is acceptable, but it is best to limit it to just one follow-up email.

Provide Links: Let's face it, not everyone knows what you have on your website. They may have heard you mention your blog or that sermons are online, but they probably do not know how to find them. An email newsletter is a great channel to get points of interest in front of those for whom you have created the content.

Take the church I attend. There are about four different locations online where someone can download the sermons from the pastor. Sermons are on the church's website, on the pastor's personal ministry site, on an iTunes channel, and on a small group's blog site. Yet, I commonly find people who do not know where to download the sermons, or do not even know you can find them online. Email will not solve that awareness problem necessarily, but it will provide the link to people at a time when they can go directly there. Giving someone directions in a bulletin is less effective than giving them a clickable link while they are already online.

Before we close out on the up-side of emails, let's focus on the ultimate benefit: You are generating engagement to your ministry. People cannot pray intelligently for your ministry if they do not know what you need. People cannot join your latest campaign if they do not know what it is. When people have information, they can get involved and take ownership.

They may miss your latest meeting and they may not be committed to reading your blog, but if they have given you permission to use their email, then you have a constant source to feed information to them. It may not help you on search engine rankings, but it is an important tactic nonetheless.

Recently broadcast television switched over from analog to digital transmission. In doing so, millions of late adopters to cable or satellite were forced to change their antennas. The government went through a huge campaign to help people change over by giving them information and providing rebates to the purchase of these new receivers. Did you ever wonder why they government was putting so much effort into the switchover?

Government knows that the best way to reach the American population is through the television. If people lose that connection, government loses that channel of communication. I am in no way implying that government is like "Big Brother"; there are many legitimate needs and much critical information that can be dispersed via TV, such as important weather warnings or a national address. My point is simply this: Having a direct line of communication with your audience is highly important. Your ministry will not find national television advertising cost effective, but having permission to email is extremely valuable.

The Pitfalls of Email Newsletters

Just as there are many benefits to email newsletters, there are also many common pitfalls. If these pitfalls are ignored, then you can actually create a worse environment for your ministry than if you never hit the send button. More than likely, these pitfalls will not hurt your search engine efforts, but they can hurt your reputation, and that could show up online for potential ministry partners to find.

CAN-SPAM

It is important to start the pitfall discussion with talk about the legal aspect to emails. CAN-SPAM is legislation in place to limit email abuse. You are a very unlikely candidate for any legal actions, but there are plenty of grey areas to these rules that could create issues for you.

The contents of CAN-SPAM revolve around three specific rules:

1. **Clear Consent to Email.** Record the date when people opt-in. Best practice for this is to have a double opt-in policy. This means whenever you are given an email address, you send an email to that address requesting confirmation. The day you receive confirmation from your email is the date you maintain for that email address.

2. **Clear Identification of Who You Are.** Leave no doubt in your recipients' minds as to who is sending the email. The "from" line needs to have the title of your ministry. Also your physical address should be within the body of the email. If you are using a third party provider to send your emails, make sure they have the ability to edit the "from" line.

3. **Clear Place for People to Opt-Out.** The most important issue is to have a clear opt-out option. It is people who are receiving email they don't want that can harm your reputation. They need to have a clear and easy way to opt-out on every email. If you are sending multiple emails (i.e. main ministry newsletter, singles, recovery, missions, etc.) then your opt-out can go to a page where they can adjust each potential newsletter. They may want to get out of the missions newsletter but keep getting the singles newsletter. They may want to stop getting everything from you. You do not want to make a mistake with this.

The Regulators of Spam

You can pretty much rest assured you will not do anything that would lend itself to litigation. But before you take it too easy, you should know that the real regulators of emails can still cause you headaches. There are a number of spam houses that maintain IP addresses of places that are known to send out spam. They then provide these lists to email providers where any emails from these IP address are blocked before they reach someone's inbox.

These lists are generated by people complaining to them about spam they have received. They then investigate the email to determine whether or not they think it is spam. This is where the guidelines become unclear. These spam houses are not regulated, so they are left to their own interpretations of spam. They thankfully catch a lot of spam and stop its activity, but they also stop many people who have just made a few mistakes.

If you send the wrong person an email and make them mad, you may get put on one of these lists. Unfortunately, there is no easy way to determine if you have been placed on one of these lists—aside from someone who wants to get your e-newsletter letting you know that they're not receiving it. Most third party emailing companies provide reports on what percentage of the people you sent emails to had opened them up (this is called "open rates"). This percentage can give you some indication if your emails are getting blocked by one of these lists.

Maintaining contact through email

Although the pitfalls needed to be addressed, email newsletters have such a great potential that they should not be avoided. When done correctly this is one of the best places to communicate with those involved with your ministry. While most of the positives and negatives are not directly related to search rankings, email newsletters do drive traffic and can drive the general attitude of your ministry. Email newsletters communicate your brand, highlight your values and addresses important issues within your ministry. Finally, if you place a newsletter archive online, it does provide more content for search engines to rank, which is definitely an additional bonus.

Chapter 7

Bringing It All Home

Why Again is this Important?

One of my professors in school started his first lecture with the question, "Who are marketers?" The answer is we all are. Everything you do leaves an impression on those around you. Therefore, as ministers of the Gospel, marketing implies being wise in the way we act to outsiders and making the most of every opportunity.[10]

Marketing is your ability to communicate what you believe. Marketing is what you do to either help or hinder that communication. Marketing is so much more than just a website and a phone book ad.

As this book focuses on websites, it is important to think through whether your website is helping or hindering the work of God through your church or ministry. Are you making the most of this opportunity? Did you spend a lot of money on a website that nobody sees?

---

10 Colossians 4:5, paraphrase

Where should I start?

The place to start, as with all things, is with prayer. Ask God what the purpose for your website is to be and what it is it to communicate. Answering these questions makes the rest of the decisions much easier. Treat this as you would anything else in the Christian life. The Christian life is not only hard, it is impossible. God designed it that way simply to make us dependant on Him to lead us through. And God, who is rich in mercy, is ready to lead you on the journey He has laid out for you. "With man this is impossible, but with God all things are possible."[11]

What Should I change on my current website?

If you do not track the traffic on your site, this would the first thing I would do. Chapter 3 goes into detail about sifting through the data, but the point I would like to reiterate here is: You cannot measure the success of a website if you do not know the data. Google Analytics is a free, detailed traffic reporting system. You can set this up quickly and start seeing the reports the very next day.

Once you have Google Analytics up and running on your site, you can determine what is working and what is not. This is the best place to start, because you can see if you are accomplishing the desired purposes of the website. Prayer is a great way to help interpret the data.

What Encouragement do You have For Me?

My encouragement for you is to dream about the people God wants to bring into your ministry.

- Who are they?
- What are they like?
- Where do they hang out?
- What do they like to do?

11 Matthew 19:26 (NIV)

As you dream about these questions and the subsequent answers, you will start to understand ways to find these people. If you were these types of people, what would you be looking for in a ministry? What words would you use to search for this type of ministry?

The question would obviously be, "Is my site addressing these felt needs? What can I add to the site to better reach these people?"

The goal here is not to make you or your ministry into something that it is not. God has a specific call on your life and ministry because of the way that He has made you. Tap into your true self. Break free from the lies and fears you have about your ministry and let God lead you into the abundant life He has available for you.

God has created you for success! This is not necessarily the success you have always thought of, because what God has planned for you is abundantly more than you can even ask or think. You are more than a conqueror and created for good works. As you seek His lead and submit your plans to His, you will have greater impact on those around you than you could ever hope possible alone.

God is seeking to find people that have faith. Faith comes from hearing. Hearing God comes from seeking Him and giving Him time to speak to you. If God calls you, He will give you what you need.

How Does This Apply to Search Engines?

The obvious question now is, "If God is in control of leading your ministry, why should you even worry about getting the marketing right?" Absolutely, you would be correct in asking this. That is why seeking God's direction is first on the list. If God is leading, He will draw people to your ministry. But, do you want to create a hurdle for these people to overcome?

God is good and merciful. He quite frequently overlooks our mistakes and continues to bless us. This is God's heart for us: Our Heavenly Father looks for ways to bless His children. The question I will pose back to you is, "Do you think God will have a greater blessing for those who seek to work with Him?"

Did you ever think that God did not call you into ministry in order to bless tons of people through it? God called you into ministry because He has greater blessings for you through your obedience. If God's greatest desire on earth was to get everyone to trust in Jesus, then…Boom! It would be done! But God's greatest desire is to be pursued and loved. His call is that we "draw near to [Him] and He will draw near to you".[12] As we seek to know Him, He will give more of Himself. Blessings are an overflow of God's reward for those who earnestly seek Him. God's children who get on board with the things on His heart will position themselves for greater blessings. Therefore, God has not done everything on His heart to do. But instead He held out on some so that He could exalt those who sought to accomplish the things that God left for us to do.

Be of good cheer. God is for you. He created you because He wants to shower you with His love and encouragement. He wants to exalt you as His child. So, if working on your website is daunting to you, realize that, if it pleases God, then He will help you accomplish it.

Closing Statements

I started this book with a quote from Richard Reising, stating that "currently, 80 to 85 percent of people are finding their church based on websites."[13] This alone states the importance, but there is so much more. Pursuing excellence in those things to which God has called you positions you for greater blessings. You will be able to greater minister to those in your church by making resources easier to find.

---

12 James 4:8a (NKJV)

13 Dolan, Thomas G. "E-Curb Appeal" Your Church Magazine. November / December 2007. http://www.christianitytoday.com/yc/2007/006/4.30.html accessed 12/26/2007.

People will be able to feel more connected to the ministry as they are more aware of its purposes and vision.

I will leave you with one last example. My name is shared by a college basketball player and by a man who was murdered by a beauty contestant. Both of these men gathered a lot of news stories, which are ranked highly with search engines because of so much coverage from reputable websites. But, with some work I have been able to secure the top 5 rankings on Yahoo! and numbers 3 & 5 on Google if you search for my name.[14] I share this for a couple of reasons. First of all, to let you know that, against all odds, this system works! Secondly, if the head of your ministry shares a name with someone who gets plenty of online coverage, you can get them in the search results with some effort. You can do this. Go out there and do it.

---

14 This search was performed on Yahoo! and Google on 9/5/2009. Results may vary on a current search.

I would love to hear your stories of success or of things you have tried. Allow me to cheer you in this process. Send your stories to me at kevin@shorterseo.com.

www.ingramcontent.com/pod-product-compliance
Lightning Source LLC
Chambersburg PA
CBHW051211050326
40689CB00008B/1275